America's Game

Cleveland Indians

Paul Joseph

ABDO & Daughters
PUBLISHING

Published by Abdo & Daughters, 4940 Viking Dr., Suite 622, Edina, MN 55435.

Cover photo: Allsport
Interior photos: Wide World Photo, pages 1, 5, 7, 8, 10, 13, 15, 16, 17, 23, 24, 25, 27.

Edited by Kal Gronvall

Library of Congress Cataloging–in–Publication Data

Joseph, Paul, 1970-
   Cleveland Indians / Paul Joseph
      p. cm. — (America's game)
   Includes index.
   Summary: Focuses on key players and events in the history of the Cleveland Indians, who have had a reputation for losing and more team names than World Series Championships.
   ISBN 1-56239-672-2
   1. Cleveland Indians (Baseball team)—History—Juvenile literature. [1. Cleveland Indians (Baseball team) 2. Baseball—History.] I. Title. II. Series.
GV875.C7J67   1997
796.357' 64771' 32—dc20   96-23090
                                                          CIP
                                                          AC

Contents

Cleveland
Indians

The Cleveland Indians are a team that is known for losing. In fact, they have had more team names than World Series Championships. The movie *Major League* portrayed a terrible franchise in Major League Baseball—and the team was the Cleveland Indians.

The Indians won two World Series in their long history. In the 1954 season they won an American League record 111 games. And those were the highlights. As great as the Indians were, most people remember the low points of this historic franchise.

Then, in 1995, things took a turn for the better. The Indians were the first team in history to win the newly formed American League (AL) Central Division.

After waiting more than 40 years, the Indians won the American League Championship and headed to their fourth World Series. Although the Series didn't end like they had hoped, the Indians showed signs of promise.

Facing page: Ace relief pitcher Jose Mesa gets set to deliver a pitch toward the plate in a game against the Detroit Tigers.

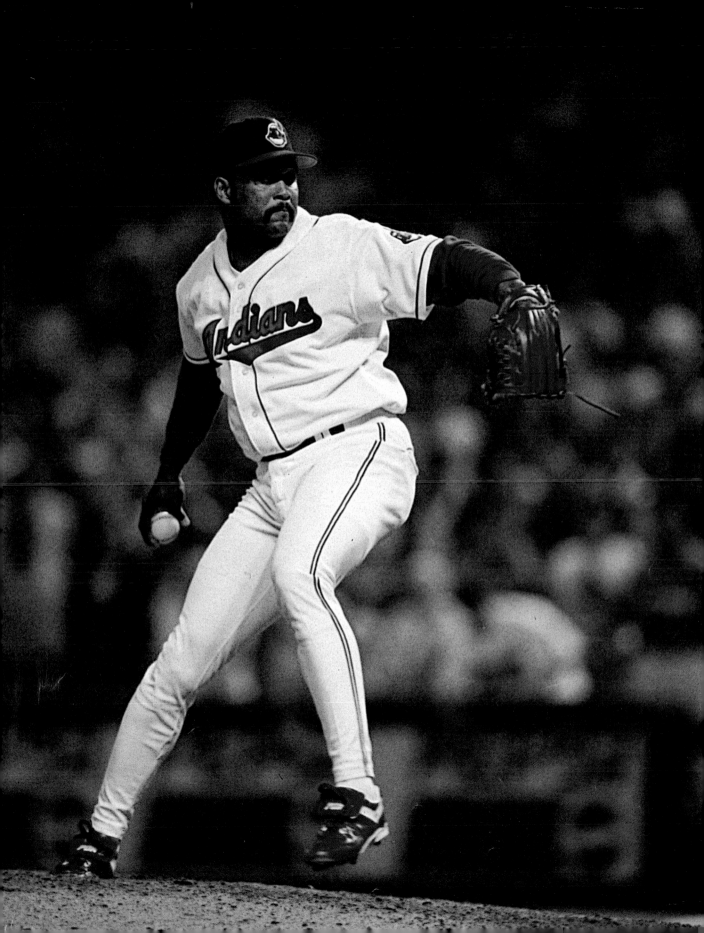

It looks as though the promise will continue. Cleveland has one of the best lineups in baseball. With solid pitching, excellent defense, and a mix of speed on the bases and power at the plate, the Indians will be the team to beat in the American League.

The future looks very bright for the Indians, even though their history has been rather dim. But the Indians have been around a long time. In fact, they even played in the first-ever American League game.

Nap Lajoie ended his 21-year career in 1916 with a .339 batting average.

The Blues And The Naps

Major League Baseball came to Cleveland when Bancroft Johnson formed the American League in 1901. He started the league with eight franchises, including the Cleveland Blues.

The first game played in the American League was on April 14, 1901, between the Cleveland Blues and the Chicago White Sox. The Blues lost in extra innings, and continued their losing ways throughout the season, finishing in seventh place.

Cleveland improved in 1902, finishing in fifth place, thanks to their new second baseman, Napoleon "Nap" Lajoie, who came over from the Philadelphia Athletics. He was as great on defense as he was on offense.

In 1903, Nap led the league with a .355 batting average and helped Cleveland move up to third place. He was so popular with the fans that the team changed its name to the Cleveland Naps.

Nap Lajoie became player-manager of the Cleveland Naps in 1904. Although the team fell to fourth place in 1903, they did win 86 games and continued to play well.

The Naps were in contention every year, but in 1908, everything came together. They had a solid lineup, led by their player-manager. First baseman George Stovall was a steady hitter with a good glove. Elmer Flick had a lifetime batting average of .315 and was a great base stealer. And finally, they had two great pitchers in Bob Rhodes and Addie Joss.

Towards the end of the 1908 season, in a crucial game against the Chicago White Sox, Addie Joss pitched the game of his career. He faced 27 batters and got each one of them out for a perfect game!

After that perfect game it seemed that the Naps had the pennant clinched, but they faltered to second place, losing games to the White Sox and the St. Louis Browns.

The following year Lajoie quit as manager to focus on playing. It worked, as he hit .324. But it didn't help the team, as they finished in fifth place.

The 1910 season looked bright for the Naps. They picked up Cy Young, the winningest pitcher in baseball history. They also acquired a great young prospect in "Shoeless" Joe Jackson. Lajoie continued to excel, finishing in second place for the batting title. But again, as a team, they finished in fifth place.

In 1911, tragedy struck the team, as star pitcher Addie Joss came down with spinal meningitis and died at the age of 31.

Cleveland began to falter, and by 1914 finished in last place. The Naps let go of Lajoie, who finished his career with the Philadelphia Athletics. Then they traded Joe Jackson to the White Sox.

Cleveland pitcher Denton "Cy" Young.

The Third And Final Name

Now that Cleveland's first real superstar and namesake was playing for somebody else, they could hardly call themselves the Naps. So they decided to name the team in honor of the first Native American to play Major League Baseball: Louis Sockalexis.

Louis Sockalexis was an outfielder for the first professional team in Cleveland, the Spiders. Sockalexis played for the Spiders in the 1800s and died in 1913. In 1915, the team got their third new name, the Cleveland Indians.

But the new name did not help. The Indians finished in seventh place in 1915 and sixth place in 1916. But there was a bright spot in 1916, the arrival of one of the all-time best center fielders: Tris Speaker.

Speaker was an excellent center fielder who could cover so much ground that it almost defied belief. In addition to his superb fielding, he was also one of the best hitters in the game. In his first year with the Indians, Speaker led the league in batting with a .386 average, ending Ty Cobb's string of nine-straight batting crowns.

The Indians also signed two dominant pitchers in Stan Coveleski and Jim Bagby, who along with Speaker led the team to third place in 1917. By 1918, Cleveland had improved to second place, only 2.5 games behind the AL Champion Boston Red Sox.

In 1919, Tris Speaker continued to be the spark plug as a player, and also took over the reigns as a manager. The new player-manager led the Indians to another second-place finish. In 1920, Cleveland shed that second-place finish and moved up to first, becoming the American League Champions.

Tris Speaker, outfielder and manager of the Indians, at Yankee Stadium in New York City.

The Indians' First World Championship

On the Indians' way to winning the AL pennant in 1920, they had to get over one of the biggest tragedies in baseball history. On August 16, the Indians took on the New York Yankees. Cleveland's shortstop Ray Chapman led off the fifth inning, crowding the plate to the challenge the pitcher, as he always did. Yankees' pitcher Carl Mays challenged him back with a fastball, hitting Chapman in the left temple.

Chapman fell to the ground unconscious, his skull fractured (in those days players did not wear helmets). He died the next morning. Chapman was the only player ever to be killed in a Major League Baseball game.

The Cleveland Indians were saddened, stunned, and shocked, but continued to play good baseball in honor of their fallen teammate. They not only played good baseball, they also played championship-caliber baseball.

After 20 seasons of play, the Indians were AL Champions. In the best-of-nine World Series (the second of only three such series) the Indians won five games to two.

Cleveland dominated the Series with the great hitting of Tris Speaker, Steve O'Neill, Charlie Jamieson, and Elmer Smith, who cracked the first-ever World Series grand slam home run.

Stan Coveleski was the pitching ace. He led the team in the regular season with an impressive 24 wins, and kept it up in the World Series. He got the win in three of the five games and finished the Series with an incredible .067 ERA.

Second baseman Bill Wambsganss etched his name into the World Series record books by turning the only unassisted triple play in Series history!

Even though the 1920 season was marked by a tragedy, the Indians played their hearts out for their lost friend and teammate. As a result, they made it one of the most emotional and memorable seasons in all of baseball history.

In 1921, the Indians still had a very talented team, and they continued to play excellent ball. But at the end of the season the Yankees stole the AL pennant, and the Indians had to settle for second place.

Cleveland began to fall in 1922, finishing in fourth place. The team finished the 1920s with some decent years but never really contended for the AL pennant. In 1932, the Indians began playing in a new stadium.

Cleveland's Municipal Stadium during the 1948 World Series.

They Built It But They Didn't Come

The Indians had been playing in League Park. Then in 1932, the city of Cleveland tried to lure the Summer Olympic Games by building Cleveland Stadium, a huge, circular stadium on the shores of Lake Erie. The stadium was mainly built for track-and-field, and could hold 78,000 people.

But the Olympics did not come to Cleveland, and the city was stuck with a huge track-and-field stadium. The Indians inherited the stadium, but the fans hated it because they were too far away from the playing field. In 1934, the team moved back to the smaller League Park.

Then in 1939, lights were installed at the huge Cleveland Stadium, and the Indians began playing night games there. Finally in 1947, the team made the oversized stadium its full-time park.

Throughout this time the Indians were up and down. Their best season was in 1940, when they had a four-game lead going into the last month of the season. Then shaky pitching took over and the Indians lost three-straight to the Detroit Tigers, who ended up stealing the AL crown by one game.

When a new owner purchased the Indians in 1946, Cleveland started to improve greatly. Bill Veeck, Jr., bought the team and became one of the great promoters of baseball. Veeck not only entertained the Cleveland fans, but he also put a winner on the field.

Outfielder Larry Doby, the first African-American to play in the American League.

A Second World Championship

Bill Veeck was well ahead of his time, and was the first to offer many free attractions to the ball park. He had fireworks, prize nights, giveaways, and used a red jeep to take the relief pitcher to the mound.

Veeck was the first American League owner to integrate baseball when he signed African-American outfielder Larry Doby in 1947. In 1948, he added Satchel Paige. Luke Easter joined the Indians in 1949. Veeck also continued to sign great, young, black prospects to minor league contracts.

By 1948, Veeck had fans in the stands with free entertainment—and his first-rate baseball team. The Indians had an all-around solid lineup.

Veteran shortstop Lou Boudreau and third basemen Ken Keltner were joined by the newly acquired first baseman Eddie Robinson and second baseman Joe Gordon. The Indians dazzling infield was matched closely by Larry Doby and Dale Mitchell in the outfield.

Rounding out the team were the men on the hill. Gene Bearden pitched his one and only good year in 1948. Bob Feller, and future Hall-of-Famer Bob Lemon, were a solid one-two combination. And 42-year-old Satchel Paige came on board that year to pick up six crucial wins and only one loss. In one of his wins, Paige pitched a three-hit, 1-0 shutout in front of a record 78,382 fans.

The race for the AL crown went down to the wire. And at the end of the regular season, the Indians were tied with the Boston Red Sox. In a one-game playoff, Cleveland was crushing the ball. Boudreau connected with two homers, and Keltner popped one dinger himself. The Indians ran away with the game and captured the AL pennant.

After waiting more than a quarter of a century to go to another World Series, the Cleveland Indians had made it back. In the 1948 World Series the Indians faced the Boston Braves.

The Braves were led by the best pitching duo in the game. Warren Spahn and Johnny Sain were masterful throughout the season and kept it up in the Series.

Satchel Paige takes to the mound during a 1948 game against the New York Yankees.

In the first game of the World Series, Bob Feller pitched a stellar two-hitter, only to be outdone by Spahn, who shut out the Indians 1-0. The Indians bounced back and took the next three games. After another good pitching performance, the Braves grabbed Game 5. Then in Game 6 the Indians got their fourth victory and were World Series Champions.

Indians' Hall-of-Fame pitcher Bob Lemon.

Cleveland

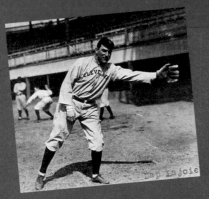

Nap Lajoie became player-manager of Cleveland in 1904.

Cy Young, the winningest pitcher in baseball history, was picked up by Cleveland in 1910.

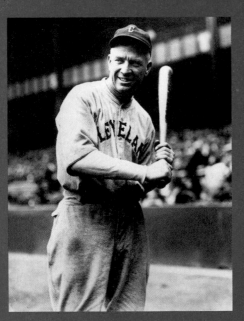

In 1916, Tris Speaker led the league in batting with a .386 average.

In 1947, Larry Doby was the first African-American to play in the AL.

Indians

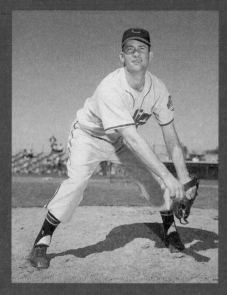

Hall-of-Fame pitcher Bob Lemon, who came to the Indians in 1941, was a 20-game winner 7 times.

Rocky Colavito crushed 20 or more homers in 11-straight seasons.

In 1986, Joe Carter hit 29 homers and had a league-leading 121 RBIs.

In 1995 Albert Belle became the first player ever to hit 50 homers *and* doubles.

Darn Yankees!

In 1949, the Indians fell to third place, and owner Bill Veeck sold the franchise because of financial difficulties. Cleveland fell one more spot in 1950 and finished fourth.

By 1951, the Indians had a good all-around lineup and an awesome pitching staff. Three pitchers registered 20 or more wins each. The team, though, had to settle for second place, behind the New York Yankees.

The 1952 season was nearly a replay of 1951. Again the Indians had three 20-game winners, and great hitters. Larry Doby led the league in homers with 32, and Al Rosen led the league in RBIs with 105. But again Cleveland couldn't get by one of the greatest dynasties of all time, the Yankees.

In 1953, Al Rosen led the Indian's offense with a .336 batting average, 43 home runs, and 145 RBIs. Again it wasn't enough. The Yankees won the AL crown and Cleveland took second.

The Indians knew that if they wanted to win the American League pennant they had to win a lot of games. And in 1954 they did just that, setting an AL record that still stands today.

The Most Wins Ever

The 1954 season didn't start out so great for Cleveland. In April, the Indians broke even. But then in May the team went on an 11-game winning streak to grab first place. From then on, they were on their way to a 111-43 season—the best ever in the American League.

Cleveland played at an amazing .721 winning percentage—one that would often guarantee the pennant. But this year, it didn't. The Yankees managed to chase the Indians until the very end of the season.

Finally in September, the Indians took command as they grabbed two victories in a doubleheader against the Yankees. In the first game, Bob Lemon pitched a six-hitter for the win, and Early Wynn did even better for the Indians as he had a three-hit victory. The Indians now had a 8.5-game lead and never looked back. The Yankees finished with an impressive 103 victories, but the effort was not good enough to beat the Indians.

After winning the AL pennant, Cleveland fans anticipated a World Championship. But after the record-setting season, the Indians couldn't muster four wins in their next seven tries. In fact they couldn't win any!

The New York Giants, led by their superstar Willie Mays, easily won the World Series, sweeping the Indians four games to none. The record-setting season ended in disappointment. All Cleveland fans could say was, "Wait 'til next year." But once again, next year was the Yankees' year as Cleveland finished second.

The Rock

In 1959, after two poor seasons, the Indians made a jump to second place, the best they would finish until 1995. They were led by a fan favorite named Rocky Colavito. The Rock hit for power rather than for average. He crushed 20 or more homers in 11-straight seasons, and hit 40 or more 3 times.

Colavito's most memorable moment came on June 10, 1959, against the Baltimore Orioles. In the first inning he drew a walk. In the third inning he barely cleared the fence for a home run.

In the fifth inning Rocky slammed a pitch 400 feet for his second homer of the day. He came to bat in the sixth and hit a homer for the third time, a 420-foot blast to dead center field.

In the ninth inning the Rock crushed his farthest homer of the day, a 425-foot shot. It was his fourth homer of the game. Only Lou Gehrig had done it before him.

Facing page: Cleveland Indians' outfielder Rocky Colavito, in a photo taken in 1967.

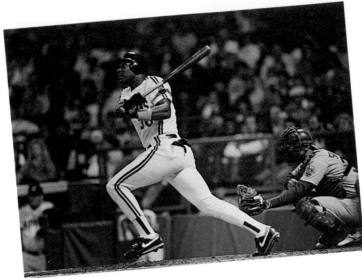

Indians' slugger Joe Carter smacks a homer in a game against the Oakland Athletics.

Stalled

After the Indians' second-place finish in 1959, the team went nowhere. The 1960s, 1970s, and 1980s were ugly for Cleveland fans. A third-place finish was as good as a pennant in those decades.

There were some bright spots for the Indians. In 1968, pitcher Luis Tiant won 21 games and had a league-leading 1.62 ERA. In 1972 and 1973, the team had Gaylord Perry on the hill, winning 24 and 19 games respectively.

In 1980, many fans believed that they had the new Rock with the arrival of outfielder Joe Charboneau. He finished the year with 23 home runs, 87 RBIs, and with the Rookie-of-the-Year Award. But that was it for him. He never came close to matching those numbers again.

In 1981, pitcher Len Barker pitched a perfect game for the Indians. He struck out 11 batters on his way to a 3-0 win. It was only the 12th perfect game in major league history. But the team was so bad that season that only 7,290 fans witnessed Barker's feat.

In 1986 Joe Carter, acquired from the Cubs, hit 29 homers and had a league-leading 121 RBIs. He continued that great pace through the 1989 season.

After the 1989 season, Cleveland traded Carter to the San Diego Padres for catcher Sandy Alomar, outfielder Chris James, and third basemen Carlos Baerga. That trade, along with power hitter Albert Belle, and rookie center fielder Kenny Lofton, had the Indians looking solid. They continued to build around that core. Cleveland added some excellent pitchers, both starters and relievers. The team was finally headed in the right direction.

Kenny Lofton beats a throw to first in a game against the Detroit Tigers.

New Home, New Division

In 1992, the Indians had a young, solid lineup, and played well, finishing the year in fourth place. The team was looking to improve even more in 1993, but disaster struck during spring training. Relief pitchers Steve Olin and Tim Crews were killed in a boating accident that also seriously injured starter Bob Ojeda. Shocked and saddened, the Indians never recovered from that tragedy, and finished the year in sixth place.

In 1994, the Cleveland Indians began playing in their new ball park, Jacob's Field. Jacob's Field looks like an old-time baseball stadium. It seats 42,000—almost half the size of the old stadium.

In 1994, a new divisional format moved the Indians into the AL Central. Cleveland played well in their new stadium and in their new division. But it was all for naught, as the players' strike canceled the season in August.

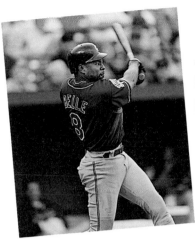

Albert Belle blasts a home run against the Baltimore Orioles.

A Pennant And A Bright Future

In 1995, Cleveland put it all together and had the best record in baseball—by 10 games. Albert Belle led the league in three categories: runs scored (121), RBIs (126), and homers (50). He also added 52 doubles to become the first player in major league history to reach 50 in homers and in doubles.

Speedster center fielder Kenny Lofton was one of the best lead-off men in the league. He finished 1994 with the most hits in the AL. In 1995, his 54 stolen bases led the league for the fourth year in a row.

The Indians had awesome starting pitching in Dennis Martinez, Orel Hershiser, and Charles Nagy, along with ace closer Jose Mesa, who led the league in saves.

The Indians raced by the rest of the AL and captured their first-ever AL Central title, winning 100 games. In the first round of the playoffs, the Indians dominated the Boston Red Sox, easily sweeping them three games to none. The Indians then played the Seattle Mariners in the American League Championship Series (ALCS) for the right to go to the World Series.

In the first two games in Seattle, the two teams split. With the next three games in Cleveland, the Indians felt confident. But Game 3 went to the Mariners. Down two games to one, the Indians bounced back and evened the ALCS. In Game 5, Cleveland came back from a 2-1 deficit to win 3-2. In Game 6, in Seattle, the Indians shut out the Mariners 4-0, and captured the ALCS. After more than 40 years of waiting, the Indians were on their way to the World Series.

The Indians faced the Atlanta Braves in one of the closest World Series in baseball history. The Braves won, four games to two, but the Series easily could have gone to the Indians. Five out of the six games were decided by one run, with one going 11 innings. The final game was also a close one, with a final score of 1-0.

For the 1996 campaign, the Indians added an excellent pitcher in Jack McDowell, and an All-Star first baseman in Julio Franco. They won their division again, but lost in the playoffs to the Baltimore Orioles.

Despite the loss of free-agent Albert Belle to the Chicago White Sox in the offseason, the Indians are still one of the best teams in baseball. They have the best rotation in the league, fronted by baseball's most intimidating lineup. They have speed, power, and great hitters, in Lofton, Omar Vizquel, Baerga, Franco, Jim Thome, Manny Ramirez, Alomar, and newcomer Matt Williams.

The Cleveland Indians' franchise hasn't had a lot of high points in their long history. But if the Indians stay healthy and play as a team, they could dominate the American League for years to come.

Glossary

All-Star: A player who is voted by fans as the best player at one position in a given year.

American League (AL): An association of baseball teams formed in 1900 which make up one-half of the major leagues.

American League Championship Series (ALCS): A best-of-seven-game playoff with the winner going to the World Series to face the National League Champions.

Batting Average: A baseball statistic calculated by dividing a batter's hits by the number of times at bat.

Earned Run Average (ERA): A baseball statistic which calculates the average number of runs a pitcher gives up per nine innings of work.

Fielding Average: A baseball statistic which calculates a fielder's success rate based on the number of chances the player has to record an out.

Hall of Fame: A memorial for the greatest baseball players of all time, located in Cooperstown, New York.

Home Run (HR): A play in baseball where a batter hits the ball over the outfield fence scoring everyone on base as well as the batter.

Major Leagues: The highest ranking associations of professional baseball teams in the world, currently consisting of the American and National Baseball Leagues.

Minor Leagues: A system of professional baseball leagues at levels below Major League Baseball.

National League (NL): An association of baseball teams formed in 1876 which make up one-half of the major leagues.

National League Championship Series (NLCS): A best-of-seven-game playoff with the winner going to the World Series to face the American League Champions.

Pennant: A flag which symbolizes the championship of a professional baseball league.

Pitcher: The player on a baseball team who throws the ball for the batter to hit. The pitcher stands on a mound and pitches the ball toward the strike zone area above the plate.

Plate: The place on a baseball field where a player stands to bat. It is used to determine the width of the strike zone. Forming the point of the diamond-shaped field, it is the final goal a base runner must reach to score a run.

RBI: A baseball statistic standing for *runs batted in.* Players receive an RBI for each run that scores on their hits.

Rookie: A first-year player, especially in a professional sport.

Slugging Percentage: A statistic which points out a player's ability to hit for extra bases by taking the number of total bases hit and dividing it by the number of at bats.

Stolen Base: A play in baseball when a base runner advances to the next base while the pitcher is delivering the pitch.

Strikeout: A play in baseball when a batter is called out for failing to put the ball in play after the pitcher has delivered three strikes.

Triple Crown: A rare accomplishment when a single player finishes a season leading their league in batting average, home runs, and RBIs. A pitcher can win a Triple Crown by leading the league in wins, ERA, and strikeouts.

Walk: A play in baseball when a batter receives four pitches out of the strike zone and is allowed to go to first base.

World Series: The championship of Major League Baseball played since 1903 between the pennant winners from the American and National Leagues.

Index